A SIMPLE

REALISTIC

APPROACH

TO GREAT

CUSTOMER

SERVICE

A Customer's perspective
on how to provide great
service for businesses of
all types and sizes.

Scott D. McCulla

TABLE OF CONTENTS

ABOUT THE AUTHOR

Scott D. McCulla was born and raised in big cities. Coming from a broken home, he started working at the early age of 11. By 13 he had his first real job in a restaurant doing cleaning, busing tables, and making French fries from whole potatoes.

That time in the restaurant would come back again as a career after a brief stint in a major hospital caring for ICU patients as a technician.

As he got older, he felt the need for a slower pace of life to pursue his goals and aspirations, and to allow for his identity to flourish.

Moving from Los Angeles to Portland, OR, Scott started working as a server and quickly advanced to manager. This management career would span some

15 years, from fast food to full service and fine dining.

After some time, a change was needed, and a new career was begun. He moved to South Carolina and started his own business in, of all things, computers.

Growing his computer career from a garage to a multi-store business, he provided service to the public and to business professionals alike. Scott felt that at the core of this business was the thought of bringing the same customer service standards from the restaurant industry to the usually introverted business of IT. This career has lasted over 20 years.

Again, feeling the need to serve others, Scott entered real estate, first as an agent with well-known companies, there taking advantage of all the training and seminars offered in this field, and then as a broker of his own company. He learned yet another meaning of customer service.

So, after some 40 years of customer service, Scott gained experience in industries from fast food to fine dining, technology, and real estate, as an employee, manager, and then business owner, all along the way as a customer and client of others, understanding how it feels to be on both ends of the spectrum. And mostly as my growth and development as a human being, I came to author this book.

At the root of genuinely great customer service is, (in my opinion), something I wrote that sums it up.

> *"Every human being deserves to enjoy things that bring them happiness. To have moments of self-indulgence. To be able to smile, laugh, and speak without judgment. To be themselves, who they truly are without fear of humiliation by others. We all should be able to find enjoyment, no matter how small, in our lives, and be the individuals we are and inspire to be. And no one has the right to steal that from us.*
>
> *Can't we let others have some enjoyment, substance, and meaning in their life?*

I hope you find some of these things I mentioned today in your life. And for others may they enjoy seeing others have that little bit of pleasure or happiness that each of us richly deserves. Today is another day of life. Live it!"

Dedication

This book is dedicated to all the hard-working wives and mothers who care for their families each and every day. They are the finest example of caring for other human beings. This book is also dedicated to all the people that are in the business of caring for other people and for the selfless dedication they have to doing so. It is an amazing quality on the part of these ones who have spent years in the service of others.

A WHOLE LOT TO DO ABOUT NOTHING. OR IS IT?

When it comes to service there may be a lot of different views as to what service really is, but it is safe to say that great customer service is perceived by the person being served, and their overall satisfaction is the final judge.

It seems in this 21 century that this is one area that has been in a broad sense in decline. People, in general, have come to expect less service or even no service. Whether it is the economizing of a company or the just plain "couldn't care less" attitude of the everyday employee, service is getting ready to be placed on the endangered list if it isn't already.

What can make the difference in the success or failure of a business is its level of service, from the way the phone is answered to the actual interaction between the server and the served. People have been molded into a closed society of communicators, meaning they feel that they have no other recourse to poor service but to tell their friends or others, and to stop buying there.

And now many people will ask first for someone's previous experience and recommendation before they are willing to experience it for themselves.

So, the power of the people is really to whom they are willing to give their hard-earned dollars. And that decision is many times dictated by a friend, workmate, or other's experience with the service they received.

So, from the mega-corporation to the mom-and-pop business, the service we provide will, over time, decide for us the success of our business. With that in mind, what are some fundamental, cheap, and easy things that can be done to correct or perfect this crucial area of success? Can this help us in our everyday jobs as well as our interaction with people in general?

The approach of this book will be the served (customer's) view and the fundamental methods that can have a profound effect. I will break it down into key areas and focus on the overall key player in this cycle which is the management. The employee has the ability to provide the stellar service that should be provided, but it is the management that sets the tone, pace, and example which has the greatest effect on the service provided by any establishment.

Whether it is a special occasion or just a need to provide the basics, people have really only a few expectations. When broken down they are:

(1) to be treated nicely, fairly, and honestly.

(2) To feel that they are appreciated for selecting you and their choice to give you their hard-earned money.

(3) to get what they are paying for, be it the product itself or the perception of value.

In our discussion, we will be using two types of businesses as a model. (1) The restaurant, and (2) the general retail establishment which sells a product or products and/or service.

I chose these because these are not only commonly visited businesses but also because they get to the very fundamental human-to-human interaction between the server and the serviced.

So, how was the service the last time you went to spend money, either eating out or just making a purchase? How did you feel about the business as a whole? Have you told anyone yet? And have you gone back again?

This gets to the heart of the experience of customer service. From the grocery store to the coffee shop, we have interaction with businesses and the individuals that represent them. If you look at your spending habits, you no doubt tend to shop at specific or regular places that you have deemed worthy of your money. For example, you choose one coffee shop over another not just for the coffee but also because of how you feel and the way you're treated when you go there. If they were to remember and call you by name, remember your order from last time, or something of the like, you tend to feel welcomed and appreciated and you will then, in turn, make this your selection of where you will then buy your next cup of coffee.

It is not as difficult as it may seem, and it can be practiced by businesses of all sizes and types. A case in point is an extra-large corporation. It may seem that it is not possible for the corporation to provide the quality of service of a mom-and-pop store.

But truth be told, it can be done, although I will add the customer perception is different. The simple ease of getting in touch with someone to help you with your questions, concern, etc. is the start.

When you call a large corporation and you do get someone to talk to, their taking time in a pleasant voice to care for your needs is the first step to providing that person-to-person service and is the start to a continuing path to success.

I remember one time I had to call a mega-corporation and I was easily directed to the department I needed. When I talked with someone in that department I was received pleasantly. When I stated why I called and my concerns they used my name and said "Mr. McCulla, let's see what we can do to get this taken care of for you." Even if I was not able to get completely what I wanted, the way the person acted as if they were my friend, and we were on the same team made me accept that fact with a smile. I felt that together we tried but weren't able to fully accomplish it nevertheless "we" tried.

So, there is my point, did that cost any substantial amount of money to provide me that service? How did I feel even though I didn't get completely what I wanted? But another question that begs to be answered is where did this person get this service skill? Was it just their personal qualities?

In doing a follow-up call, I found that I was directed to another person working in that department and they were just as accommodating.
So, this must have come from a company "mentality," not necessarily a company policy or a chance individual!

What do I mean? Well, we can tell people to be nice; we can list the consequences for their failure to do so. But in my experience that usually has limited effect. It is when we create a "mentality," an acknowledgment of the standards of care, an understanding of how the company feels about the people that buy from them, and their expectations of the quality of that care and how serious that commitment to the care of that person, client, or customer really is. So, it is where all employees are in unison with the mindset of the company's authority or management in how they are to deal with their customers' "people" and why.

Thus, we come right to management. Sometimes we see a company make an effort by changing the names of so-called services or patrons. For example, in a restaurant, they may call a customer a "guest," or their customer service "hospitality." In a conceptual view that is a step in the right direction, but why? Because it is creating a mindset, a mentality of how the customer, guest, or client is viewed. Ergo, the effort to care for them is hopefully reflected in all levels of our staff and that starts from the top on down, and from the beginning of a person's employment. Let's spend a few minutes on that particular aspect.

HIRING RIGHT. FROM THE START!

A company/business hires an employee to provide direct contact with the customer, be it a cashier, server, host, clerk, etc. This really applies to any position, but let's focus on the direct customer contact. How important is that job? Well, that person is the face, voice, attitude, care, or reflected standards of the company, so then is that how it is viewed?

Many businesses feel that answering the phone, and direct face-to-face contact with the customer is an entry-level position, when in fact it is one of the most important positions in the company. If this is not the thinking of the upper management, then it is presumed that they have failed in providing the quality of service that makes for long-lasting successful businesses.

I remember a young woman I hired to be an order taker and cashier. After spending time explaining to her how important this position was and how strongly I felt about it, we provided her with the needed training. Afterward, I stood back from a distance and watched her and how she interacted with our customers. After observing her at length I noticed she hardly smiled. So, after her shift, I sat her down and asked her how she liked the position and working for the company she replied, "I like it." I asked her if she enjoyed caring for our customers. She said, "Oh yes!" I then asked her why she didn't smile, and her answer taught me something. She said, "I do smile." I said, "You do?" She said, "Oh yes, all the time," so I told her my observations.

She didn't believe me; she was convinced she was always providing a great big smile when in fact she wasn't.

So, what did this teach me? This little anecdote teaches that not everyone has the needed qualities to be the face or voice of our business. And we need to be observant and concerned enough to make the necessary adjustments. So afterward I moved her to a different position where she thrived and blossomed, and she felt more job satisfaction as a result. But the fact of the matter is that her previous position was not the position I felt she was best placed in and thus I was not getting and doing the best for neither our customers nor my employee. What she did with her new position had a profound impact on the good of our customers and she received accolades for her work.

So fundamentally, it is our view of the very role of each and every person we employ from the janitor to the general manager that we need to examine. Not everyone is suited for every position in our business, and we need to have a clearly defined picture of the quality of service we wish to provide is and then find and hire the correct person for the position. We then need to be observant and vigilant in monitoring that service or care and making needed changes when necessary.

So, in so many words, we are talking about customer perception or how people who engage us in transactions (do business with us) perceive that experience. This experience is shaped in many ways even before the customer comes face to face with our service representative. What do I mean?

IS WHAT YOU SEE WHAT YOU GET?

My wife and I decided to go out to dinner one evening. As we drove down the busy street looking for a place to eat and we made a decision. So, we turned in and the first thing we noticed was that the building didn't look like it was in good condition and as we drove to the back of the building to park there it was.

We saw four employees in the back of the building by the garbage smoking, horsing around, with unkempt uniforms. It was at that point we then changed our minds and left for another selection. What was it that made us change our minds?

It was a poor first impression: employees outside smoking, horsing around, unkempt uniforms, and the building was not maintained. We could only imagine the prompt service we would be getting and the clean environment we would be eating in. and that is nothing to say of the sanitary care of our food. Thus, this business lost our business that night but not just for the night, also for good.

And here is where we venture into another area of quality of service "customer perception." Customer perception is a difficult thing to measure. For example, in that same situation, I just mentioned if it was in the inner-city and there was a reputation or mystic of the inner-city place with the best "whatever" in town then perhaps we may have ignored the first impression based on all the positive comments of those we trust or view as in the know.

But that doesn't make it right and it still was a hurdle we had to jump to move forward. So human perception can vary but overall, people like to eat in a clean environment and have the secure feeling that their food will be prepared as such and that they will be given the attention they are entitled to. There are many things that affect the perception of the people we serve. Some are visible like the story above or the not so visible or should I say not so prominently visible.

Let me give you some comparisons. First, how your building looks and how employees conduct themselves are very important to that all-important first impression. There is what I call a series of impressions all along the way, for example, the appearance of the first contact person. Is their dress neat clean, and orderly?

What about their personal preferences? I know that some may enjoy the multiple nose rings or earrings, but is their personal preference going to be the impression we want to give our guests?

Then there is the atmosphere. The music: is the volume at a comfortable level for the visitors or is the volume for the employee's enjoyment? What about the type of music?

I remember one time we were dining out at a nice family restaurant, upscale and from the outside to the inside very well done and nice impression. We were greeted by friendly employees and were seated. But as we tried to decide what to eat from the menu the music was not only loud, but it was screeching-screaming music. It got to such a point I asked to speak to the manager and complained about how much the music was a displeasure to our visit. Well happily the music volume went down, and the selection was changed to something more suitable for this dining experience.

But getting back to the point of impressions. The series of impressions all along the way from the first contact person including the atmosphere, all build a perception or image in the minds of the customer of how the business overall is operating. Are all the staff busy, and efficient? Does the operation seem to be clean and orderly?

Again, the issue of cleanliness comes to the fore. We many times hear our friends or others say, "If the bathrooms are clean then most likely the kitchen is too."

And that does hold true in most cases, but it is the perception that an unclean area reflects the business's overall concern and care for hygiene and cleanliness. And sometimes it is not just the obvious places like the bathroom.

I remember one occasion sitting down to enjoy a meal with my wife when I reached for the ketchup and got it on my hands because it was all over the bottle as they didn't wipe it down after the previous guests, and then I reached for the salt and pepper or as they say in the south the sale & peppa. Anyway, they were greasy and cloudy like they had not been changed in some time. Need I say more about what was going on in my mind?

I couldn't help to think the whole time we we're sitting there, about how the salt and pepper shakers were so unclean and they were only about 18 inches from our (guests, customers) face and touch.

So, I could continue to talk about cleanliness but let me just put it this way: Everyone loves to be in a clean environment. Sure, you may hear someone say, I'm not comfortable in a sterile place.

But I did not say sterile I said clean. And everyone likes to enjoy clean things and they expect it as well in virtually every place, thing or person. And think of how much money is spent on cleaning and keeping things clean.

Yet if our business does not have the awareness or thoughtfulness to create a clean environment, it will be for not that we spent not only money but ultimately it will be reflected in lower sales and eventually no sales at all. And this takes us back to management!

IS THERE A MANAGER IN THE HOUSE?

I believe, and I tell people as well, that when you have a bad experience in a place of business it was the management's fault. If the management had a firm and consistent method relating their standards and expectations, then that would be reflected in their employees. If the manager followed up and was diligent in ensuring that the highest level of care was provided or if a manager is kind, fair, and firm in his setting the standards of what is acceptable and what is not, as well as his expectations as to how things are to be done and what the businesses priorities are.

This will more than not result in a pleasant experience for their customers, and subsequently higher sales and profitability. But we have all heard of the horror stories if we haven't experienced them firsthand. But the quality of the management staff is the single most critical and unreliable area of any business.

What do I mean? Well, the manager's job you could say is to interpret and effectively implement company policy and standards. To ensure the customer experience is the best it can be and to maintain the property in a condition that would complement that. Too many times we find managers that are poorly trained and poorly selected for their position. I have talked with and trained many managers, and what I have found is a void in many cases of basic management skills.

I could categorize the management skills in these ways. **The screamer:** this is the manager that thinks that yelling at their staff is a display of people management as well as their position of authority. I have found this to be completely ineffective and it is an embarrassment to the manager, as not only the staff but any customer in earshot would no doubt have a negative view of that person.

The Desk Jockey: this style is when the managing of others and the business operation is done from the office or behind the desk. Now need I say more as to how effective this is. Not only is this ineffective but it sets a poor example and sends the distinct message that avoiding the customer is the right thing to do.

Then there is **The Lost One:** I always get a kick out of this style. This is the style where the manager just kind of wanders around, not telling or giving anyone any real direction or they seem oblivious to the customers and their experience. Similar to the desk jockey there is the customer avoidance syndrome that is on display for all to see.

Then you have **The Good Buddy**: this manager never wants to have to be the disciplinarian but tolerates what is not being done and then usually gets fired because the job performance of others reflected so poorly on his or her management abilities.

Then we have **The Balanced, Diligent One:** this is the one that comes to work with an action plan and goals they wish to get accomplished that shift. They are reasonable but firm in ensuring their staff performs to their best and provides the best care for each and every customer. They communicate their expectations and follow up to ensure that it is being carried out.

They also communicate and provide a correction that may be necessary to not only ensure customer care but also to provide the needed development of their staff to perform their best as well.

THE EXTRA MILE

I need to tell you some experiences that will bring home the point of what we are now about to discuss. It is what not to do and by contrast what should be done things of customer service. No doubt you may have all heard about the department store that a customer entered to purchase some shoes and the store was out of that style. The sales representative asked the customer to please wait he would be right back.

While the customer waited, he ran down to another store that carried that style of shoe, he then purchased them and returned to his store and sold them to the customer. While that may be a great story of customer service it does set an example of what caring for the customer really means and by extension the company mentality that would allow such acts of service to be considered or let alone take place.

In contrast, I went to a fast-food restaurant one winter day to have a brief lunch and wanted a cup of tea which was on their menu, and I had had there on a number of prior occasions. I was told that they didn't have hot tea, so I said it is on your menu and I had it here before and they then replied, "we are out of tea bags." While I stood there deciding what else to drink, I couldn't help but notice that across the street was a supermarket.

So, I mentioned to the cashier that perhaps she should mention to the manager that a quick run across the street to buy a box of tea bags would make me and perhaps other customers happy. I was acknowledged with a reluctant, "I will mention it" reply and a quick, "next."

I guess what was so frustrating to me was not that they didn't have tea bags, but that they did think to make the effort to go get some which were conveniently close, I might add. After all, it was a winter day and hot tea was in demand.

Let me tell you one more just to drive the point home. I ordered a receiver for my home entertainment system after much research and excitement. After 35 days I started to have an issue with the video, so I called tech support, and we troubleshoot the problem only to conclude I needed to send it to their repair center.

So, I did, which cost me $25 in shipping charges to do so, and I was without the centerpiece for my entertainment center for about 6 weeks. When I received it back, I set it all up, and again I had trouble with the video. So, I called customer service, and this time I was told I needed to send it back to the repair center and they would send a call tag. So again, I sent it to the repair center, and I was without my receiver for about 4 weeks.

I received it back again and I set it up only to find the remote wouldn't work. So, I called tech support, and they concluded that the remote sensor was defective and, you guessed it, I should send it to the repair center for the third time.

To make a long story short, I emailed the national service manager and was told I needed to send it to them to confirm it was defective and that they would replace it.

I emailed the president of the company and never received a reply. So, I emailed the national service manager again and refused to again be without my receiver for weeks on end and felt I should be sent a replacement in exchange for the unit I had. Well, needless to say, it didn't happen, and what is even more insulting was he resent me the same email response he had earlier?

So, I moved on and will never buy from them again even though it was a very good product by most standards. But what made this so bad?

It was the horrible customer service skills and the endless rules on handling matters that only brought satisfaction to the company but dissatisfaction to me the customer. I told this story to a friend, and he related to me his own experience with a printer manufacturer that sent him a replacement right away after his first product issue.

Now I know that it may be cost-prohibitive to send a replacement to everyone that has any issue, but after a reasonable amount of inconvenience, their care for their customer should supersede their policy that only leads to frustration and anger eventually leaving the customer with their only recourse, to tell as many as possible about their bad experience just as I have done with you right now (smile).

So, the question is, are we willing to be reasonable, and see the value in just taking care of the customer?

Not only does it make them happy, but it saves a lot of time and negative energy on your employee's part as well. You decide!

ONE MORE "BEFORE" THE ROAD: ALL I WANT TO DO IS PLACE AN ORDER!

The other day my family, friends, and I went to a local restaurant for dinner. As we began to order, a friend who was dining with us asked for just a salad instead of a complete meal package deal that was offered. The manager proceeded to tell us how we can't have the salad separately. He continued to explain that if we get the salad a la carte, we can't eat it here that we would need to get it to go. So, I replied fine, we wanted to eat here, so she will get the entire meal. Then she asked if coffee came with the complete meal package, and he proceeded to tell her no we don't do that anymore and that you have to purchase it separately, again I replied fine just place the order please I am getting confused and frustrated.

Then after all that lo and behold, as we began to eat our meal the waiter comes and asked if we want any complimentary coffee to go with our meals. We asked if there was an additional charge for our coffees and he said no, "it's complimentary."

After he had left, we were bewildered, looking at each other as if we were in some kind of twilight zone.

So why am I sharing this story with you and what main point can we learn from this? Well, first our feelings about going to this restaurant are firmly negative, we didn't need a third degree about the things we ordered but a simple answer and perhaps an attempt to accommodate us would have made a difference and had been nice. Then the coffee debacle, we didn't mind paying for a beverage if required but again the negative approach all about what we can't do or what can't be done for us.

And then to have the staff completely unaware of the supposed coffee policy change and doing what we had thought was the policy, to begin with, was the final straw in our decision never to go back.

So, my point is, if you're so afraid of every penny that you can't explore an accommodation, you're in the wrong business; you should be an accountant in an office counting pennies not in the service business, in this case, a restaurant.

And finally, if you are going to make a policy change and be firm about it then roll it out to all involved so that the policy is at least consistent.

So, from the two experiences above we can see a clear point made about the need to care for people in a kind, caring, empathetic and appreciative way, after all, if we are in the service industry, we are really in the people business! So, what is that thought leading to?

IF THEY WERE YOUR FAMILY

I think that if everyone we cared for in our service career was our immediate family then maybe we would get better service. For example, I think if every woman you served was your beloved wife, or every man was your beloved husband, perhaps we would be providing more thoughtful caring service. Or maybe it was your favorite grandmother or - father or your closest friend and confidant then we would be more attentive, patient, caring, thoughtful, accommodating, and more.

Well, shouldn't everyone be treated that way? After all, they are someone's mother, father, grandmother or -father, special close friend! If you had to meet the children of such individuals after you had been serving them, would you be able to say you treated them like they were my close family or friend or feel the need to hide?

Have you ever thought in your 8-5 or 9-6, or whatever you work, that many of the people we deal with are coming to see us because they either are in need of or want our service and we can make that a memorable or regrettable experience?

It might be best illustrated this way. You're the server at a restaurant and an older couple is coming there for a 50th wedding anniversary meal. Their income may be such as this was a planned and a very special occasion that normally they wouldn't be able to splurge or afford. But they have come to you and you're not attentive, you're forgetful, or worse yet you're impolite and curt. The food takes too long and comes out wrong or cold. What have you done?

Because of your failure to carry out the job, you're being paid for, or the attitude you have toward your job, you just made this special moment one to forget, not remember. And it becomes just another disappointment for them in their quest for some measure of happiness in this world filled with pressure, stress, and attacks on family and other human institutions.

You may say hey that is an awful heavy thing to lay at my feet, I can't help all the issues and unpleasant experiences people have in life. Well, I say to you, you can at least do your part in helping one or two people at a time. After all, they are paying for it, and you are being paid to do it!

So then let's stop being selfish and do our jobs the way we should be doing them, the way we agreed to do it. And if you're not up for caring for your job or caring for others, might I remind you of what I mentioned earlier about finding a different job? Perhaps one more suitable to your disposition or performance!

This leads me to what normally is at the root of this attitude or approach to our jobs.

People's personal lives:

I just wanted to spend just a moment on this subject of our employees' personal lives. Sad to say it has been more than once that I have gone into a business and found an employee dealing with some domestic issue on the phone while I stood and waited. Or the "conversation" between employees that I had to wait until they finished before I was even acknowledged. Frankly put, I am sorry about the many situations that arise in the lives of employees some being unavoidable and some even tragic.

And these situations usually are far and few between but what I am addressing is the never- ending drama where the workplace is the festival grounds for their personal issues. This always ends in the customer getting neglected and the attitude displayed by the employee being should I say less than desired.

So, employees need to keep it outside and off the clock. And managers need to deal with it and be consistent, reasonable, and fair in handling the matter. Perhaps the employees need some time off to do their catching up on the local gossip.

Nevertheless, this is happening all too often, and the management allows it to happen. Once I even saw the manager take my order out of frustration because two cashiers were talking about personal matters. I think that comes under the "good buddy" management style, no?

THE ART OF SAYING NO!

I would be remiss if I didn't address the other aspect of great customer service. That of the art of saying NO!

Now let me first say a fundamental truth. No one likes to be told no.

From infants to the elderly. Humans don't like to be told no and added truth, they don't like to wait either, anyway.

You have heard that the customer is always right. To a degree, I agree with that old adage. But there are times when out of what is right, fair, and honest we must say no to a customer or client. The key in all of this is how we say it, not that we did.

The art of saying no is when you can tell your customer no and they respect you for it. Meaning they understand and respect you more for it as a businessperson. One with morals, principles, and standards. This then instills in them (silently perhaps) the thoughts and feelings that you are an honorable business they can trust and have confidence in.

And hopefully that the same standards, principles, etc. of your business will be practiced in ultimately all your dealings with them.

So here is a brief outline of how to do that: First, a warm attentive expression of acknowledgment, letting them know you're not able to do that.

Second, then a reasonable, clear, and understandable explanation.

Third, then listening and empathizing with their position but reaffirming the company's stand on the matter.

Fourth, if some compromise can be reached then we should strive to do that.

Now, this is not related to our giving poor service that a customer or client is upset and wanting. But when their requests or demands are not reasonable, fair, or honest.

Now a detour worth taking.

CLEAR MARKETING MESSAGE

This one always tickles me. I don't know how many times I have seen advertising and wondered what does that have to do with this company, better yet when you are not even sure what company it is talking about. It seems that advertising agencies may be running out of creative ideas or the staff to do so.

Time and time again I am left wondering what did this company just spend all this money on? And we don't even know what it was they were saying.

Now granted, I may not be the sharpest knife in the drawer, but that makes my point even stronger. If even a simple mind can't get it, then was there a point, to begin with? And this trickles all the way down to even the menu. It seems that more and more I can't find and figure out how to decide what I want to eat at an eating establishment because I can't find it on the menu.

The menus today are confusing, and the items are scattered and not grouped together, it seems.

Now, this may be me or a ploy to get me to buy a meal deal or some other type of arranged meal, which is more profitable but the fact I felt frustrated and uncomfortable about my order and was left with the feeling I had to settle for something that I really didn't want to begin with is a problem.

To me, it is a dangerous marketing strategy if you want to call it that. I hear the comment that research, and polling were done. Well, let me say this to all of you marketing and advertising professionals.

If a giant software company can spend perhaps hundreds of millions of dollars in research, marketing, etc., on a release of new software that only results in frustration and eventual rejection by their consumers. You had better rethink your methods and data.

For example, I installed some software and started to use it only to find that it had all sorts of frustrating features that I didn't want and didn't feel I needed. I had to ask, didn't someone in all those studies and polls sit down and use it and say hey this is annoying, and I don't like it? Or maybe it is all the professionals that want to look like they have this great idea, and it was nothing more than a marketing plan for a career boost.

The facts speak for themselves. Simply put, here is what our marketing message should do. Tell the consumer what you are selling, how it benefits them, the cost, and where it can be found.

And if we are manufacturing something then try using it ourselves without the hovering designer explaining all the reasons why this or that is such a great feature. If you can't simply sit and use something for its intended purpose, then it is designed wrong. I won't even spend time about the instructions or lack thereof that are given or not with such supposed wonderful products.

THE ELECTRONIC AGE

Everything we discussed thus far applies as well to this electronic age or age of technology.

For example, I received a multi-fold advertisement in the mail. I sat at my desk for about a minute just trying to figure out how to open it without tearing it apart. I don't think I need to tell you what happened next. Yes, the garbage.

So, all that effort and yes cost was wasted because someone or many someone's didn't even think about how the recipient would experience the presentation of the marketing material.

Which leads me to websites. With all the skill sets and all the money spent on web marketing and websites, it amazes me how some very large businesses make it so hard to do business with them through the web, as well as how some others clearly get it.

A story to drive home the point.

I wanted to buy some tires, so I went to one of the major tire company websites and I needed, in this case, to buy a tire by size, not by the automobile type.

The only option I had was by auto type, I couldn't find anywhere where I could buy the tire by the tire size.

I found it frustrating and insulting that they would make it so difficult.

I then proceeded to another company's site where I could buy by auto type, tire size, and any other way I wanted. It not only was convenient, but it gave the complete total and allowed me to book an appointment.

Subsequently, I did just that and had a great buying experience and was so pleased I am writing about it right this minute.

DON'T THINK YOU'RE SMARTER THAN YOUR AUDIENCE

One thing I think has not been addressed when talking about electronic business is the many games that companies play thinking they are smarter than their audience or potential customers! I am not sure who they are listening to, but they need to get down to ground level and get more realistic feedback.

For example, you go to a website, and you see a link that says you can download something or continue in an article. And you end up someplace else and can't find what you were intending and then you are plastered with advertisements and many of which are false or misleading. Extremely frustrating!

What are you intending to sell? Frustration? Anger?

It doesn't take much to know you're getting a bad reputation. And in time will spell goodbye to your online audience "Customers."

So, knock off the games and play it straight. Make it easy and forthright. Then you can expect your audience yes customers to not only buy again but also recommend!

You also may think you're fooling your customer but over time they not only figure out what you've been doing but then have solidified a completely negative attitude not just toward the misleading practice but also the company as a whole.

One case in point is have you ever called a company and were told due to high call volumes you can expect to wait longer than normal wait times.

Now, this usually happens when you're trying to call tech or product support, it seems to never be a problem when you're trying to call sales.

But just think when company after company tells you when you call their support line that you are going to have an extraordinarily long wait time to reach tech or product support or whatever it may be. I cannot help but think either they are understaffed in that department or their product etc. has so many problems that a ton of people are calling.

It amazes me that nobody thinks that through, that really what they're saying is we will sell you our product (that's why the sales line is usually free or gets answered promptly), but we won't support our product or at least try to avoid supporting our product by having to make you wait extraordinarily long wait times for a department that should be at least equally as available as the sales department.

Then there is to me the ultimate insult and that is companies that provided almost no access to customer service. One that comes to mind is the largest social media network that has no way to speak with one of its representatives in any way shape or form.

You have no choice but what they've given you that is to look at their training or reference materials and hope that not only can you understand it but that following their directions will actually work.

I am astonished and on the other hand, appalled that more and more companies are making it that difficult for their customers (from whom they generate a very handsome profit) to contact them when they have valid issues. Eventually, this is going to come back around, and it usually does, when the honeymoon with this social media company or this new tech gadget or fashion quickly becomes old, and their revenue-generating customers discard them as they move on to new and more innovative services or products.

So, in this age of technology the principle of completely thinking through the process, from start to finish on how we will provide a great business experience applies.

THE WORD OF MOUTH HAS JUST GOTTEN LOUDER.

Also, in this electronic age has the old word of mouth gotten amplification by means of social media. Here's one for the little guy.

Now your clients/customers have an outlet to express their dissatisfaction with poor service or products.

And since this can be done with relative ease then it is even more important than ever to provide the best service and product possible.

Now, rather than asking someone for their experience they can see reviews and read what that experience has been. Granted they don't always reflect the actual experience and I think for the most part many people take that into consideration.

Nevertheless, the power of the people's voices is getting louder and can be heard farther than ever.

It is like a camera in an office that the employee forgets is there. If a business is not providing the best service possible each and every time, then any flaw can be made public.

So, this means that businesses small or large need to have service procedures and protocols clearly set out so that in each interaction the goal of great service is provided.

ONE FOR ALL AND ALL FOR ONE

You may have found something in this book that may be useful, or you may have said our situation is different. Well, quite frankly it's not.

If you're providing a product or service to people, then it applies to you no matter what the size of your business. This also applies to businesses of all types, when we begin to recognize that we need to sober up in regard to the quality of service we are really providing then maybe we will take some clear, firm, measures to take our quality of service to the level that not only we as a business owner or company president would like, but even more importantly to a level of service that our customer, client, end user (whatever you may call that person) feels is quality care, yes quality service.

So, let's talk about some suggestions that all those in authority or under authority should exercise.

- Come to the realization that you have chosen this as your career and that you will do your best at it.

- Start your day with a to-do list/action plan. This can be a simple few items to start. Be productive and have a clear list of things you plan to get accomplished that day.

- Be friendly, kind, reasonable, and fair in your dealing with your staff and customers.

- Set clearly defined goals not just for yourself but have clearly communicated and defined goals for your entire staff and or company. And do not accept mediocre performance.

- Monitor continuously the quality of service that your business is providing. Listen to how the phones are answered; the greetings are displayed, and so on. If you are in upper management then you need to have systems in place to monitor these things from afar for yourself.

- Always find ways to challenge your staff to excel and grow in their jobs or careers. Reward those under your supervision, find things that they have done that are right and commend them. Commend them even for their ideas and willingness to contribute to the betterment of the operation or business. When correction is necessary then do so as promptly as possible at the proper place and time.

- Then leave the person with their dignity and an opportunity to regain your approval.

- Stay out of your chair and in the field or out with your customers as much as possible. Granted you may need to spend a lot of time in your office to care for your duties. But make it a goal to get out into the field on a regular basis. See, hear, and listen to the day-to-day care of your most valuable commodities.

Your customers and your staff!

- Be open to ideas and areas in your job performance where you can grow. Do a daily reflection on your performance and the quality of your work. What areas are you beginning to become stagnant in or complacent in, and what areas have you grown overconfident in perhaps?

- Work and organize your job duties in such a way that you can spend time with your family and friends as well as some quality time in solitude with yourself.

If the quality of care in our businesses is going to get better, we need to wake up and do some serious self and business evaluation.

We need to be willing to say, "I fail in this area, and I do well in this one." Then get serious and pursue your plan to improve in that area that requires attention.

When we are so out of touch with our business that we don't really know what most of our customers think about our business, then we are in need of an overall change. And I said most of our customers because we may talk with one and think that all is well when in fact it is not. This situation is all too common in institutions of all kinds, and I see it every day.

Great service should not be the rare, outstanding news flash but the everyday workings and production of our companies.

This subject of serving others properly extends far beyond our working environment. It will reflect in our personal lives as well. From our marriage mates to extended family and friends. Everyone deserves to have a measure of personal attention shown to them.

JUST AS A FRIENDLY REMINDER

Every human being deserves to enjoy

thing that brings them happiness. To have moments of self-indulgence. To be able to smile, laugh, and speak without judgment.

To be themselves, who they truly are without fear of humiliation by others.

We all should be able to find enjoyment in our life no matter how small and be the individual we are and inspire to be. And no one has the right to steal that from us.

The question is, can we let others have some enjoyment, substance, and meaning in their life?

I hope you find some of these things I mentioned here in your life. And for those of us in the service profession may we enjoy seeing others have that little bit of pleasure or happiness that each of us richly deserves. Today is another day of life. Live it!

The author

CONCLUDING THOUGHTS

There is much more to add to this book, and I am sure as you read it your own experiences come to mind both good and bad.

But it is really more than just the subject of service that is discussed here. It is civility, the basic human concern for others. The manners, and graciousness that are becoming so rare with the human interaction of today's world.

Perhaps this book can help do something to heighten the awareness of a slowly degrading mindset toward the service of others.

Now, this is not to say all. There are many outstanding service businesses as well, who I might add "get it!"

But as I mentioned earlier it shouldn't be a pleasant surprise when we get great service. But it should be the everyday mindset that the bottom line is we are dealing with other human beings.

When we approach our jobs with that in mind, it makes dealing with them a much more meaningful and pleasant experience.

More about the author and acknowledgments.

Scott D. McCulla is the owner and operator of the following current and former businesses.

AAORP REALTY: Residential and Commercial.
THE SOUTH CAROLINA REAL ESTATE ASSOCIATION.
SUPERLATIVE DINING: Business service analysis.
JAVA MEDIA SOLUTIONS: Digital Signage
GREATPRICEPC: Computer stores.
MCM NETWORK SYSTEMS: B2B IT
COLUMBIA SMOOTH JAZZ.COM: Internet radio.

Scott D. McCulla has many years of public speaking experience. Including very large audiences. He is available by invitation to do so.

I wish to thank all those that have read this book and all those who helped in making this book possible. Thank you all very much!

www.ingramcontent.com/pod-product-compliance
Lightning Source LLC
Chambersburg PA
CBHW060644210326
41520CB00010B/1734